WORLD'S GREATEST DAD JOKES

CLEAN & CORNY KNEE-SLAPPERS FOR THE FAMILY

WORLD'S GREATEST DAD JOKES

ADRIAN KULP

ILLUSTRATIONS BY JEREMY NGUYEN

ROCKRIDGE
PRESS

Interior and Cover Designer: Eric Pratt
Art Producer: Samantha Ulban
Editor: Erin Nelson
Production Editor: Ruth Sakata Corley

Illustrations © Jeremy Nguyen, 2020

Author Photo Courtesy of © Jen Mayer Kulp.

ISBN: Print 978-1-64739-664-0 | eBook 978-1-64739-388-5
R0

For my kids, Ava, Charlie, Mason, and Evelyn. Never forget all the laughter that we've shared, even if it was at the expense of your dear old dad.

CONTENTS

Introduction

Like many dads, mine was always prepared with a zinger up his sleeve—something simple and corny that would have us belly-laughing from the back seat.

You never knew when it was coming. It could be on the open highway during a family road trip or in his pickup on the way to go fishing at the lake. Sometimes, it was while he was cutting our hair in the driveway, or, horrifyingly, when he was dropping off my girlfriend and me at the movies. You'd cringe, just waiting for that telltale moment: "Didja hear the one about..."

Whether it was something smart and creative, a pun, or even a riddle, dad jokes were his special way of connecting with us. Sure, at one point they made us blush with embarrassment, but there was always something genuine, honest, and funny about them.

What I've only recently come to appreciate is how my dad's jokes, and the humor we shared, shaped not only my career in comedy, but also my future relationships. My wife used to think I was the funniest guy alive. (I love you, honey.) Then we got married and I needed a new audience, so we started poppin' out kids. One at a time, they learned to laugh with and at me. This is my love language—the dad joke. It can be yours, too.

This collection of jokes is for every dad, mom, and kid out there. Here's to the groans, knee-slappers, eye rolls, and gut busters you'll share with those you love to laugh with most.

What did the buffalo say to his son when he dropped him off at school?
"Bison."

1

CHEESE WHEEL Q&A

HOW MANY DADS DOES IT TAKE TO SCREW IN A LIGHTBULB? JUST ONE, BUT HE WANTS TO KNOW WHO'S BEEN LEAVING THE LIGHTS ON. . .LIGHTBULBS DON'T GROW ON TREES, SONNY! THE CLASSIC Q&A JOKE IS THE CHEESEBALL YOUR KIDS (AND COWORKERS) CRAVE, BASICALLY SHELF-STABLE AND RIPE FOR TRADING AT RECESS OR THE WATERCOOLER.

What do you call a cheese with no friends?
Provolonely.

Why were the utensils stuck together?
They were spooning.

Why did Beethoven get rid of his chickens?
All they said was "Bach, Bach, Bach."

When is a door not a door?
When it's ajar.

What date night costs just 45 cents?
A 50 Cent concert featuring Nickelback.

**What do you call a parade of rabbits
hopping backward?**
A receding hareline.

Why don't scientists trust atoms?
Because they make up everything.

How do you make a chicken salad wrap?
Add some fresh beets.

How do you keep a bagel from getting away?
You put lox on it.

How many apples grow on a tree?
All of them.

Why can't you explain puns to kleptomaniacs?
They always take things literally.

"KIDS ARE DEFINITELY THE BOSS OF YOU. ANYONE WHO WILL BARGE INTO THE ROOM WHILE YOU ARE ON THE COMMODE IS THE BOSS OF YOU. AND WHEN YOU EXPLAIN TO THEM THAT YOU'RE ON THE COMMODE AND THAT THEY SHOULD LEAVE BUT THEY DON'T? THAT'S A HIGH-LEVEL BOSS."

—TINA FEY

What sits at the bottom of the sea and twitches?
A nervous wreck.

Why don't skeletons ever go trick-or-treating?
They have no body to go with.

What do you call a bear with no teeth?
A gummy bear.

Why don't the melons get married?
Because they can't elope.

What does Charles Dickens keep in his spice rack?
The best of thymes and the worst of thymes.

When does a joke become a dad joke?
When it becomes apparent.

What did the bald man say when he was gifted a comb?
"Thanks, I'll never part with it!"

Why did the chicken go to the séance?
To get to the other side.

How do you set up a staff meeting in space?
You planet.

What do you call someone with no body and no nose?
Nobody knows.

What did the pirate say on his 80th birthday?
"Aye, matey."

What does a zombie vegetarian eat?
"GRRRAAAAAIIIINNNNS!"

What time did the man go to the dentist?
Tooth hurt-y.

**How many tickles does it take to
make an octopus laugh?**
Ten tickles.

Can February march?
No, but April May!

What is faster: hot or cold?
Hot, because you can catch a cold.

Why was the man unhappy with the Velcro he bought?
It was a total rip-off.

Why do bees have sticky hair?
Because they use honeycombs.

What does an angry pepper do?
It gets jalapeño face.

What do microscopic organisms use to call each other?
Cell phones.

Why did the Clydesdale give the pony a glass of water?
Because he was a little hoarse.

What is the sound of a witch's vehicle?
Brrrroooom, brrrroooom.

Why are elevator jokes so classic?
They work on many levels.

IT'S A DAD THING

IF YOU'RE OLD ENOUGH TO CRITIQUE
WHAT I PUT IN YOUR LUNCH, YOU'RE
OLD ENOUGH TO MAKE IT YOURSELF.

What did the police officer say to his belly button?
"You're under a vest."

Why do chicken coops only have two doors?
If they had four, they'd be chicken sedans.

Dad, did you get a haircut?
No, I got them all cut.

How do you get a squirrel to like you?
Act like a nut.

Why don't eggs tell jokes?
They'd crack each other up.

Why couldn't the bicycle stand up by itself?
It was two-tired.

Dad, can you put my shoes on?
No, I don't think they'll fit me.

Why can't a nose be 12 inches long?
Because then it would be a foot.

Dad, can you put the cat out?
I didn't know he was on fire.

MOM: How do I look?
DAD: With your eyes.

Why did the scarecrow win an award?
She was outstanding in her field.

A gift for you

Happy fathers day old man! From Andrew

What's black and white and goes around and around?
A penguin in a revolving door.

How do you make a Kleenex dance?
Put a little boogie in it!

Why can't you hear a psychiatrist using the bathroom?
Because the "P" is silent.

What do you call an elephant that doesn't matter?
An irrelephant.

What do you get from a pampered cow?
Spoiled milk.

What's black and white and blue?
A depressed zebra.

How do lawyers say goodbye?
"Sue ya soon!"

What's the best way to watch a fly-fishing tournament?
Live stream.

What's an astronaut's favorite part of a computer?
The space bar.

What did the drummer call his twin daughters?
Anna One, Anna Two.

How did Darth Vader know what Luke got him for Father's Day?
He felt his presents.

What Nevada city do all dentists visit?
Floss Vegas.

Does anyone need an ark?
I Noah guy.

How do you make holy water?
You boil the hell out of it.

What do you call a man with a rubber toe?
Roberto.

What do you call a fish with two knees?
A two-knee fish.

Why do you never see elephants hiding in trees?
Because they're so good at it.

**What did the caretaker say when they
jumped out of the store cupboard?**
"Supplies!"

**Did I tell you about the time I fell in
love while summersaulting?**
I was head over heels.

Why did the coffee file a police report?
It got mugged.

Where do vowels live?
In an A-frame home.

MOM: Stop being ridiculous, just be yourself.
DAD: Make up your mind!

What did the fried rice say to the shrimp?
Don't wok away from me.

What do you call a man who can't stand?
Neil.

What do you call cheese that isn't yours?
Nacho cheese.

What did the grape do when it got stepped on?
It let out a little wine.

Why are cats lucky but bad storytellers?
They have nine lives but only one tale.

Why was the belt sent to jail?
For holding up a pair of pants.

What do you call a baby monkey?
A chimp off the old block.

Do you think glass coffins will be a success?
Remains to be seen.

What happens when a frog's car dies?
He needs a jump. If that doesn't work, he has to get toad.

Why did the bee get married?
Because she found her honey.

What do you call a can opener that's broken?
A "can't opener."

SON: Dad can you tell me what a solar eclipse is?
DAD: No sun.

IT'S A DAD THING

RAISING KIDS IS LIKE
NAILING JELLO TO A TREE.

DAUGHTER: I'll call you later.
DAD: You can just call me "Dad."

How does a meteorologist go up a mountain?
They climate.

What did one snowman say to the other?
"Can you smell carrots?"

What do you call an alligator in a vest?
An in-vest-igator.

Why does Waldo wear stripes?
He doesn't want to be spotted.

What do elves learn in school?
The elf-abet.

Why is no one friends with Dracula?
Because he's such a pain in the neck.

**What did the snail say when it was
riding on the turtle's back?**
"Wheeee!"

Why did the invisible woman turn down the job offer?
She couldn't see herself doing it.

Why don't big cats play poker?
Too many cheetahs.

Why couldn't the pirate play cards?
Because he was sitting on the deck.

What did the hat say to the scarf?
"You hang around, and I'll go ahead."

What did the right eye say to the left eye?
"Between you and me, something smells."

What do you call a duck that gets all As in school?
A wise-quacker.

**What did the dry cleaner say to
the impatient customer?**
"Keep your shirt on."

How do you catch a whole school of fish?
With bookworms.

What does a spy do when she gets cold?
She goes undercover.

What's orange and sounds like a parrot?
A carrot.

How does the moon cut his hair?
Eclipse it.

How do you keep a bull from charging?
Take away his credit card.

How do you fix a cracked pumpkin?
With a pumpkin patch.

What does a baby computer call his father?
Data.

**What do Kermit the Frog and Oscar
the Grouch have in common?**
They both have the same middle name.

Why did the kid cross the playground?
To get to the other slide.

Why did Mickey Mouse take a trip into space?
He wanted to find Pluto.

How did the cats end their fight?
They hissed and made up.

Why can't you play hockey with pigs?
They always hog the puck.

Why did the cookie cry?
Because his father was a wafer so long!

What do you call a snake wearing a hard hat?
A boa constructor.

What did one horse say to the other at the dance?
You mustang-o with me.

GRANDPA: I think I have a "dad bod."
DAD: To me it's more like a father figure.

Why did the student eat his homework?
Because the teacher told him it was a piece of cake.

What has four wheels and flies?
A garbage truck.

Why are frogs so happy?
They eat whatever bugs them.

What do you get when you cross a centipede with a parrot?
A walkie-talkie.

What is brown, hairy, and wears sunglasses?
A coconut on vacation.

Why is the grass so dangerous?
It's full of blades.

What do you call a hippie's wife?
Whatever her name is.

Why can't you give a pushover a balloon?
He'll let it go.

**What did Obi-Wan say to Luke when
he kept dropping his food?**
"Use the fork, Luke."

**Why do bananas have to put on sunscreen
before they go to the beach?**
They might peel.

Where do baby cats learn to swim?
The kitty pool.

Why are spiders so smart?
They know how to research on the web.

How can a leopard change his spots?
By moving.

**What did the photon say when asked
if she needed to check a bag?**
No thanks, I'm traveling light!

What did the duck say when she bought ChapStick?
"Put it on my bill."

What does a cow use to do math?
A cow-culator.

What's brown and sounds like a bell?
Dung.

Did you know that milk is the fastest liquid on earth?
It's pasteurized before you even see it.

Why are skeletons so calm?
Because nothing gets under their skin.

What did one ocean say to the other ocean?
Nothing, they just waved.

Why does everyone enjoy being around the volcano?
It's just so lava-ble.

MOM: I'm washing the car with our daughter.
DAD: Shouldn't you use a sponge?

What kind of music do the planets listen to?
Nep-tunes.

What did Mars ask Saturn?
"Hey, can you give me a ring sometime?"

What did the big flower say to the tiny flower?
"Hey there, bud."

What did the baby corn ask the mama corn?
"Where's my popcorn?"

Why couldn't the poppy seed get off the hill?
It was on a roll.

Why do bears have hairy coats?
Fur protection.

Why did the onion have a hard time telling jokes?
There were too many layers.

Why did the coach go to the bank?
To get her quarter back.

What did the fisherman say to the magician?
"Pick a cod, any cod."

If Iron Man and Silver Surfer teamed up, what would they be called?
Alloys.

Why did the computer have no money left?
Someone cleaned out its cache.

What's a computer's favorite snack?
Microchips.

Why was the robot so tired after his road trip?
He had a hard drive.

What do you say to a pepper who thinks he knows more than you?
Serrano!

What do you call a cheese with depression?
Blue cheese.

What does the ocean use to do its laundry?
Tide.

**What did the greedy businessman
say when it was cold outside?**
Jacket up.

Why do birds fly to warmer climates in the winter?
It's much easier than walking.

What creature is smarter than a talking parrot?
A spelling bee.

What did one plate whisper to the other plate?
Dinner is on me.

What kind of tree fits in your hand?
A palm tree.

Why did the math book look so sad?
Because of all its problems.

Should you have your family for Thanksgiving dinner?
Best to stick with just turkey.

Why didn't the chef finish the gravy?
He would have, but he ran out of thyme.

Didja hear about the shoplifter?
He was found squashed under a shop.

2

DIDJA KNOW, KID?

THE PERFECT WAY TO MORTIFY YOUR KID AT THE
BREAKFAST TABLE, BREAK UP A SIBLING FIGHT, OR
HOLLER OVER THE FENCE TO YOUR NEIGHBOR. DIDJA
HEAR THE ONE ABOUT THE GUY WHO STOLE 10
BARS OF SOAP FROM THE SUPERMARKET?
HE MADE A CLEAN GETAWAY.

Didja hear the joke about paper?
Never mind—it's tearable.

**Didja know which US state has
the smallest soft drinks?**
Minisoda.

Didja hear about the guy who invented Life Savers?
They say he made a mint.

Didja hear about the book on antigravity?
It's impossible to put down.

**Didja hear about the mathematician
who's afraid of negative numbers?**
She'll stop at nothing to avoid them.

**Didja hear about the place where average
things are manufactured?**
It's called the Satisfactory.

Didja hear about the two guys who stole a calendar?
They each got six months.

Didja hear about the circus fire?
It was in tents.

Didja hear about the restaurant on the moon?
Great food, no atmosphere.

Didja see they made round bales of hay illegal in Wisconsin?
The cows need a square meal.

Didja hear about the pizza joke?
Never mind, it's too cheesy.

Didja hear about the giant who threw up?
It's all over town.

Didja hear about the guy who cut off the left side of his body?
He's all right now.

Didja hear about the pregnant bedbug?
She's going to have her baby in the spring.

Didja hear about the two smartphones that got married?
The reception was great.

Didja hear about the claustrophobic astronaut?
She just needed a little space.

Didja hear about the scientist obsessed with a boiling pot of water?
He considered it an esteemed colleague.

Didja hear the rumor about butter?
Well, I'm not going to spread it!

"THE TWO THINGS IN THE WORLD WE ALL SHARE ARE LAUGHTER AND PAIN. WE'VE ALL GOT PROBLEMS. THE LEVELS OF THOSE PROBLEMS VARY, BUT WE'VE ALL GOT PROBLEMS. WHEN YOU CAN TAKE THINGS THAT ARE PAINFUL AND MAKE THEM FUNNY, THAT'S A GIFT—TO YOU AND YOUR AUDIENCE."

—KEVIN HART

**Didja hear about the guy who invented
the knock-knock joke?**
He won the no-bell prize.

**Didja hear about the actor who fell
through the floorboards?**
He was just going through a stage.

**Didja hear about the power outlet who
talked smack to the power cord?**
He thought he could socket to him.

**Didja know the first French fries weren't
actually cooked in France?**
They were cooked in Greece.

Didja hear about the popular cemetery?
People are just dying to get in there.

Didja hear about the pencil with two erasers?
It was pointless.

Didja hear about the Italian chef?
She pasta way.

**Didja hear about the man who fell
into an upholstery machine?**
He's fully recovered.

**Didja hear about the young cat who
went to work for the Red Cross?**
She wanted to be a first aid kit.

IT'S A DAD THING

NINETY PERCENT OF PARENTING
IS JUST THINKING ABOUT WHEN
YOU CAN LIE DOWN AGAIN.

Didja hear about the famous artist who was arrested?
Turns out he was framed.

Didja hear about the baguette at the zoo?
It was bread in captivity.

**Didja hear about the man who put on a clean
pair of socks every day of the week?**
By Friday he could hardly get his shoes on.

Didja hear that the price of duck feathers has risen?
So now even down is up.

Didja hear about the man who stole a truckload of eggs?
Apparently it was a big yolk.

**Didja hear about the man who gave
up his job as a fishmonger?**
He said it was making him shellfish.

Didja hear about the cat who drank three bowls of milk?
He set a new lap record.

Didja hear about the two ghosts who fell madly in love?
It was love at first fright.

**Didja hear about the new movie in which a beautiful
girl falls in love with a very ugly loaf of bread?**
It's called *Beauty and the Yeast*.

Didja hear about the stonemason's son?
He was a chip off the old block.

**Didja hear about the baby ghost who
tried out for the football team?**
He heard the coach say they needed a little team spirit.

**Didja hear about the guy who stayed up
all night to see where the sun went?**
It finally dawned on him.

**Didja hear about the music store
that was robbed last night?**
The thieves made off with the lute.

Didja hear about the banana who snored loudly?
He woke up the whole bunch.

**Didja hear that the man who invented the
clock has written his autobiography?**
It's about time.

**Didja hear about the man who
works in the watch factory?**
He just stands around and makes faces all day.

Didja hear about the paranoid bloodhound?
He was convinced that certain people were following him.

Didja hear about the new deodorant?
It's called "Vanish." You spray it on and become invisible,
so no one knows where the smell is coming from.

**Didja hear about the two cyclops who were
always arguing with each other?**
They could never see eye to eye about anything.

Didja hear about the neurotic octopus?
He was a crazy mixed-up squid.

Didja hear about the predatory fish?
He was a loan shark.

Didja hear about the dentist and the manicurist?
They are always fighting tooth and nail.

Didja hear about the man who opened a flea circus?
He started it from scratch.

**Didja hear about the two satellite
dishes that got married?**
The wedding was out of this world.

**Didja hear about the bicycle that went
around attacking people?**
It was a vicious cycle.

**Didja hear that the local food factory is not
going to make sausages any longer?**
They're long enough already.

**Didja hear about the detective who became
famous after solving crimes by pure chance?**
He was called Sheer Luck Holmes.

Didja hear about the rich rabbit?
He was a million-hare.

**Didja hear about the piglets who wanted to do
something special for their mother's birthday?**
They threw a sowprize party.

Didja hear about the horse that's been in 27 movies but never gets recognized anywhere?
He just does bit parts.

Didja hear about the woman who named her racehorse Turnip?
She wanted a horse people could root for.

Didja hear about the dog who ate nothing but garlic?
His bark was much worse than his bite.

Didja hear about the woman who couldn't find a singing partner?
She ended up buying a duet-yourself kit.

Didja hear about the man who stole a truckload of prunes?
He's been on the run for the last month.

Didja hear about the pigeon who wanted to buy a famous London landmark?
He put a deposit on Big Ben.

Didja hear about the kidnapping?
He woke up.

Didja hear about the man who became thirsty when he visited family in Vancouver?
He drank Canada Dry.

Didja hear about the dating agency for chickens that went bankrupt last week?
They couldn't make hens meet.

Didja hear about the very intelligent monster?
He was called Frank Einstein.

Didja hear about the man who listened to the match?
He burnt his ear.

Didja hear about the musical ghost?
He wrote haunting melodies.

Didja hear about the fool who keeps going around saying "no" anytime someone asks them a question?
(No.) Oh, it's you!

Didja hear it took Mozart hours to finish his homework?
He had too many notes.

IT'S A DAD THING

MY KID IS TURNING OUT TO
BE EXACTLY LIKE ME. WELL
PLAYED, KARMA, WELL PLAYED.

Didja hear the one about the statistician?
Probably.

Didja hear about the man who was tap dancing?
He broke his ankle when he fell into the sink.

Didja hear about the animal hotel that has an exclusive accommodation for squirrels?
It's called The Nutcracker Suite.

Didja hear about the guy who went bankrupt in the dry-cleaning business?
He said he was all washed up.

Didja hear about the yachtsman who had his arm cut off?
He wanted to sail around the world single-handed.

Didja hear about the extremely vain actor?
Every time he opened the refrigerator door and the little light came on, he would bow.

Didja hear about the child who was named after his father?
They called him Dad.

Didja hear what happened to the guy who couldn't keep up payments to his exorcist?
He was repossessed.

Didja hear about the man who went to the bank to borrow money?
The bank teller said the loan arranger was out at the moment, and the man said, "I'm trying to buy a house, not fight outlaws!"

Didja hear about the man who almost drowned in a bowl of muesli?
A strong currant pulled him under.

Didja hear about the guy who decided to become an editor?
He wanted to make a long story short.

Didja hear about the restaurant on Mars?
The prices are astronomical.

Didja hear about the very wise mirror?
It had a lot of time to reflect.

Didja hear about the boating business in an attic?
Sails were through the roof.

Didja hear about the prayer in an overcoat and sunglasses?
It was a blessing in disguise.

Didja hear about the tailor who is very forgiving?
He'll always cut you some slack.

Didja hear about the clock that started doubting its choices?
It was having second thoughts.

Didja hear about the woman who called off her wedding after an organ transplant?
She had a change of heart.

Didja hear about the tightrope walkers who got married after two weeks of dating?
They really fell head over heels.

Didja hear about the artist who couldn't figure out why no one would buy his art?
He was drawing a blank.

Didja hear about the pair of average numbers that went bankrupt?
They were living beyond their means.

Didja hear about the surgeons who were madly in love?
They knew each other inside and out.

**Didja hear about the marathoner
who lost the 30-yard dash?**
She was really disappointed, but she'll win in the long run.

Didja hear about the angry paleontologist?
She had a bone to pick.

**Didja hear about the guy who quit boxing
and became a bestselling writer?**
He was making money hand over fist.

**Didja hear about the woman who
didn't appreciate her statue?**
She really took it for granite.

Didja hear about the busy dad who had four sons?
He worked son up to son down.

Didja hear about the lumberjack who got a promotion?
Now she's a branch manager.

Didja hear about the orange who went to court?
He was there on appeal.

Didja hear about the woman who smelled really good?
She used both her nostrils.

**Didja hear about the man who tried
to stay awake for 24 hours?**
He made it to 23 and called it a day.

Didja hear about the hungry clock?
It went back four seconds!

Why are cats so good at video games?
Because they have nine lives.

3

PUNNY YOU SHOULD ASK

SOME MIGHT SAY THE PUN IS THE HIGHEST FORM OF
DAD JOKE, TO WHICH I SAY, BE CAREFUL UP THERE!

What do you do if your dog chews a dictionary?
Take the words out of his mouth.

**What did the hot dog say to the bun
that beat her in a race?**
I relish the fact that you've mustard the
strength to ketchup to me.

Why do fish live in salt water?
Because pepper makes them sneeze.

Where do mice park their boats?
At the hickory dickory dock.

Where did the sheep go on vacation?
The Baaaahamas.

What do you call a thieving alligator?
A crook-o-dile.

How do you say "bye" to a curly-haired dog?
"Poodle-oo!"

**What did the judge say when the skunk
came into his courtroom?**
"Odor in the court!"

What day do chickens fear the most?
Fry-days.

Why did the elephant stay in the airport?
It was waiting for its trunk.

What did the horse say when it fell?
"Help, I've fallen and I can't giddy-up!"

What did the therapist say when a horse walked in with tears in its eyes?
"Why the long face?"

What do you call a horse that lives next door?
A neigh-bor!

What time does a duck wake up?
At the quack of dawn.

Who stole the soap out of the bathtub?
The robber duck.

What did the dog say when he sat on sandpaper?
"Ruff!"

Why did the poor dog chase his own tail?
He was trying to make ends meet.

What animal keeps the best time?
A watchdog.

What happens when it rains cats and dogs?
You can step in a poodle.

Why are dogs like phones?
Because they have collar IDs.

What do you get if you cross fireworks with a duck?
Quite the firequacker.

What has fangs and webbed feet?
Count Quackula.

What was the goal of the detective duck?
To quack the case.

Why can't a leopard hide?
Because he's always spotted.

Why do plants hate math?
It gives them square roots.

Why did the student get upset when his teacher called him "average"?
It was a mean thing to say.

Why is the obtuse triangle always so frustrated?
Because it is never right.

Why can you never trust a math teacher holding graph paper?
They must be plotting something.

Why was the equal sign so humble?
She knew she wasn't greater than or less than anyone else.

What do you call a number that can't stay in one place?
A roamin' numeral.

What do you call brothers who love math?
Algebros.

**A guy was admitted to the hospital with
eight plastic horses in his stomach.**
His condition is stable.

The mozzarella made a bunch of bad jokes in a row.
It was grating.

Why is electricity flunking out of history class?
It only knows about current events.

What did the forager say to the other forager?
"We're in this to gather."

Why did the ghost need orthotic shoe inserts?
His sole needed more support.

What did France say when London looked sad?
"UK?"

**Did you hear about the sponge who
never asked any questions?**
He was self-absorbed.

I started growing a lemon tree.
It's given me a real zest for life.

What do you call immortal trash?
Garb, because it's ageless.

IT'S A DAD THING

WHEN YOUR DAD VOICE IS SO LOUD
THAT EVEN YOUR NEIGHBORS BRUSH
THEIR TEETH AND GET DRESSED.

What do you call the number seven and the number three when they go out on a date?
The odd couple (but they're both in their prime).

Why should you never talk to pi?
Because it'll go on and on and on forever.

Parallel lines have a lot in common, so why is their relationship doomed?
Unfortunately, they'll never meet.

What's the best way to flirt with a math teacher?
Use acute angle.

How do you stay warm in any room?
Just huddle in the corner, where it's always 90 degrees.

Why is six afraid of seven?
Because seven eight nine.

Why *did* seven eat nine?
Because you're supposed to eat three-squared meals a day!

Why does nobody talk to circles?
It's hard to see the point.

A man just came at me with milk, cream, and butter.
How dairy.

I am a big fan of whiteboards.
I find them quite remarkable.

I just burned 2,000 calories.
That's the last time I leave brownies in the oven while I nap.

The future, the present, and the past walked into a bar.
Things got tense.

I accidentally swallowed some food coloring.
The doctor says I'm okay, but I feel like I dyed a little inside.

Don't interrupt someone working intently on a puzzle.
Chances are, you'll hear some crosswords.

**Did you hear about the man who
went for a swim in Paris?**
He was in Seine.

**My girlfriend told me she was leaving me because
I keep pretending to be a Transformer.**
I said, "No, wait! I can change."

I'm glad I know sign language.
It's pretty handy.

eBay is so useless.
I tried to look up lighters and it gave me 13,749 matches.

RIP boiled water.
You will be mist.

My lazy-eyed wife and I just got a divorce.
I found out she was seeing someone on the side.

**I recently heard about a mannequin
who lost all of his friends.**
He was too clothes-minded.

A book just fell on my head.
I've only got myshelf to blame.

For Halloween, we dressed up as almonds.
Everyone thought we were nuts.

I can't believe I got fired from the calendar factory.
All I did was take a day off.

A short psychic broke out of jail.
She was a small medium at large.

I wondered why the Frisbee was getting bigger.
Then it hit me.

**My first job was working in an orange
juice factory, but I got canned.**
I couldn't concentrate.

A courtroom artist was arrested today.
The details are sketchy.

A Spanish magician was doing a magic trick.
He said, "Uno, dos . . ." and he disappeared without a trace.

I've written a song about tortillas.
It's a rap.

**I own a pencil that used to belong to William
Shakespeare, but he chewed it a lot.**
Now I can't tell if it's 2B or not 2B.

Two cheese trucks ran into each other.
De-brie was everywhere.

Are monsters good at math?
Not unless you Count Dracula.

I met the man who invented the windowsill.
He's a ledgend.

A cellist refused to go to a boxing match.
He couldn't stand violins.

**People don't like having to bend
over to get their drinks.**
We really need to raise the bar.

I lost my mood ring the other day.
I'm not sure how to feel about it.

Some clown opened the door for me this morning.
That was a nice jester.

**Police have arrested the world
tongue-twister champion.**
I imagine he'll be given a tough sentence.

I need to stop drinking so much milk.
It's an udder disgrace.

I put a new freezer next to the refrigerator.
Now they're just chilling.

My new girlfriend works at the zoo.
I think she's a keeper.

I'm taking part in a stair-climbing competition.
I need to step up my game.

I used to build stairs for a living.
Business was up and down.

**What's the last thing Grandpa said
before he kicked the bucket?**
"How far do you think I can kick this bucket?"

How did the Spanish-speaking legume introduce itself?
"Hola, soybean."

When is an Irishwoman having a good time?
When she's Dublin over with laughter.

I put my dog in the oven, but it's okay.
He's pure-bread.

Have you ever tried folding a fitted sheet?
It's easier if you cut corners.

What do you call an American bee?
A USB.

Two windmills are standing in a field and one asks the other, "What kind of music do you like?" The other says, "I'm a big metal fan."

What is a sailor's favorite letter?
They all love the C.

What do cows read to their kids at bedtime?
Dairy tales.

Why did the pianist alienate his roommates?
He was always losing the key.

Never make a business deal with a guitar player.
They'll just string you along.

I once had a teacher who compulsively looked right at the sun.
She couldn't control her pupils.

Why did the driver name her racecar Radish?
She didn't put too much thought into it,
she just knew it couldn't be Beet.

A weightlifter failed a math test, then placed third in a national lifting championship.
He was all bronze and no brains.

What's it like to have tea with a sunbeam?
Delightful.

Why was the shoe such a good detective?
She could always tell when something was afoot.

Why was the apple dressed in a fancy gown?
She was getting ready for the Gala.

How do ancient Greek gods say they're sorry?
They Apollo-gize.

I sat down at a restaurant and the server immediately asked if I wanted dessert.
I told him that's the last thing I want.

How do bunnies propose to each other?
Whatever they do, they have to get 24 carrots.

Why did the burritos delay an important decision?
They needed to taco 'bout it.

How do watermelon seeds wish each other a happy Valentine's Day?
"You're one in a melon."

What did the dried fruit say to his dad?
"You did a grape job raisin me."

IT'S A DAD THING

PARENTING IS A LOT LIKE
THE BAR SCENE: EVERYONE'S
YELLING, EVERYTHING'S
STICKY, IT'S THE SAME MUSIC
OVER AND OVER AGAIN, AND
OCCASIONALLY SOMEONE PUKES.

Why did the sharks get married?
They wanted to make it o-fish-al.

**What does an owl say when she hears
a name she doesn't recognize?**
"Who?"

Why did the marsupial get the job?
She met all the koala-fications.

Why was the barista at a loss for words?
There were certain things he couldn't expresso.

Why did the woman fall into a well in broad daylight?
She didn't see that well.

Why do octopuses win every fight?
They're well-armed.

What do you call a cow on stilts?
High steaks.

I heard a story about a haunted refrigerator.
It was chilling.

Becoming a vegetarian is a big missed steak.

Show me a piano falling down a mineshaft
and I'll show you A-flat minor.

I wasn't originally going to get a brain
transplant, but then I changed my mind.

I had a job tying sausages together, but
I couldn't make ends meat.

A friend of mine tried to annoy me with bird
puns, but toucan play at that game.

Long fairy tales have a tendency to dragon.

I used to work in the woods as a lumberjack, but
I just couldn't hack it, so they gave me the ax.

I was going to share a vegetable joke, but it's corny.

I was hoping to steal some leftovers from
the party, but my plans were foiled.

Most people are shocked when they find
out how bad an electrician I am.

The first time I got a universal remote control,
I thought, "This changes everything."

I couldn't quite remember how to throw a
boomerang, but eventually it came back to me.

No matter how much you push the
envelope, it'll still be stationary.

I would make jokes about the sea, but they're too deep.

I'm already feeling numb from these corny jokes,
and math puns make me feel number.

My garbage can speak, but all it does is talk trash.

I tried to do spring cleaning, but it sprung away from me.

Some people can't even recognize an instrument when
it's right in front of them, accordion to a recent study.

I like my friend Custard, but sometimes it
can be hard pudding up with him.

I tried to make dinner reservations at the
library, but they said they were booked.

I think it's hilarious to put clown makeup on the left side of my face, but not everyone sees the funny side.

You can't wear glasses when you play football because it's a contact sport.

Origami is pretty fun, but it's a lot of paperwork.

Some people like elevators, but I find that they drive me up a wall.

My aunt took a photo of me, but I made her give it back.

I trust that tiger because I know she isn't lion.

I asked my dad to make me a sandwich and he put me between two slices of bread.

Wearing cowboy clothes is ranch dressing.

Towels tell jokes, but they're all pretty dry.

The postal service is a mail-dominated industry.

I wouldn't recommend eating clocks because it's time-consuming.

This guy I know drove his expensive car into a tree and found out how a Mercedes bends.

IT'S A DAD THING

IT'S TRULY AMAZING THAT
AS HUMANS WE CAN LEARN
SOMETHING NEW EVERY
DAY. FOR EXAMPLE, EVERY
THURSDAY I RELEARN THAT
OUR DAUGHTER HAS BALLET
FROM 5:00 TO 6:00 P.M.

4

KNEE-SLAPPIN' KNOCK KNOCKS

KNOCK-KNOCK JOKES ARE AN AMERICAN CORNBALL
STAPLE, AND IT'S NO MYSTERY WHY THE KNOCK KNOCK
STILL WORKS. A PLAY ON WORDS MEETS AUDIENCE
PARTICIPATION MEETS DAD HUMOR? KNOCK, KNOCK.
WHO'S THERE? BRILLIANCE.

Knock, knock.
Who's there?
Water.
Water who?
Water you doing, just open the door!

Knock, knock.
Who's there?
Mustache.
Mustache who?
**I mustache you a question, but
I'll shave it for later.**

Knock, knock.
Who's there?
Leon.
Leon who?
Leon me when you're not strong.

Knock, knock.
Who's there?
Annie.
Annie who?
Annie thing he can do, she can do, too.

Knock, knock.
Who's there?
Lena.
Lena who?
**Lena a little closer, and I'll
tell you another joke!**

Knock, knock.
Who's there?
Quiche.
Quiche who?
Can I have a hug and a quiche?

Knock, knock.
Who's there?
Adore.
Adore who?
Adore is between you and me, so please open up!

Knock, knock.
Who's there?
I am.
I am who?
Don't you even know who you are?!

Knock, knock.
Who's there?
A leaf.
A leaf who?
A leaf you alone if you leaf me alone.

Knock, knock.
Who's there?
Hike.
Hike who?
I didn't know you liked Japanese poetry.

Knock, knock.
Who's there?
A little old lady.
A little old lady who?
I didn't know you could yodel.

Knock, knock.
Who's there?
Cargo.
Cargo who?
Cargo beep, beep and vroom, vroom.

Knock, knock.
Who's there?
Ice cream soda.
Ice cream soda who?
Ice scream soda people can hear me!

Knock, knock.
Who's there?
To.
To who?
I think you mean "to whom."

Knock, knock.
Who's there?
Candice.
Candice who?
Candice joke get any worse?

Knock, knock.
Who's there?
Interrupting sloth.
Interrupting sloth who?
(10 seconds of silence) Slooooooooth.

"I'D WALK THROUGH FIRE FOR MY DAUGHTER.
WELL, NOT FIRE, BECAUSE IT'S DANGEROUS.
BUT A SUPER HUMID ROOM. BUT NOT TOO HUMID,
BECAUSE MY HAIR."

—RYAN REYNOLDS

Knock, knock.
Who's there?
Banana.
Banana who?
Knock, knock.
Who's there?
Banana.
Banana who?
Knock, knock.
Who's there?
Orange.
Orange who?
Orange you glad I didn't say, "Banana"?

Knock, knock.
Who's there?
Alex.
Alex who?
Alex-plain when you open the door!

Knock, knock.
Who's there?
Olive.
Olive who?
Olive next door. Hi, neighbor!

Knock, knock.
Who's there?
Hawaii.
Hawaii who?
I'm fine, Hawaii you?

Knock, knock.
Who's there?
June.
June who?
**June know how long I've been
knocking out here?**

Knock, knock.
Who's there?
Spell.
Spell who?
W-H-O.

Knock, knock.
Who's there?
Oscar.
Oscar who?
Oscar silly question and get a silly answer.

Knock, knock.
Who's there?
Conrad.
Conrad who?
Conrad-ulations on your knock-knock joke.

Knock, knock.
Who's there?
Anita.
Anita who?
Anita go to the bathroom, let me in.

Knock, knock.
Who's there?
Owls say.
Owls say who?
Yes, they do.

Knock, knock.
Who's there?
Cash.
Cash who?
No thanks, but I'd love some peanuts.

Knock, knock.
Who's there?
Dwayne.
Dwayne who?
Dwayne the bathtub, I'm dwowning.

Knock, knock.
Who's there?
Ya.
Ya who?
No thanks, I use Bing or Google.

IT'S A DAD THING

IS IT RUDE TO START ASKING MY
MOTHER-IN-LAW FOR CHILDCARE
FEES? HER CHILD IS A HANDFUL
AND I DON'T WORK FOR FREE.

Knock, knock.
Who's there?
Control freak.
Control freak who?
**You know what, let's just start this over
and I'll do the whole thing myself.**

Knock, knock
Who's there?
Control freak.
Contro-
Okay, who are you calling a "control freak"?!

Knock, knock.
Who's there?
Billy Bob Joe Penny.
Billy Bob Joe Penny who?
**Really? How many Billy Bob Joe
Pennies do you know?**

Knock, knock.
Who's there?
Theodore.
Theodore who?
Theodore wasn't open, so I knocked.

Knock, knock.
Who's there?
Alec.
Alec who?
Alec it when you ask me questions.

Knock, knock.
Who's there?
Keith.
Keith who?
Keith me, my thweetheart.

Knock, knock.
Who's there?
Double.
Double who?
W!

Knock, knock.
Who's there?
Beats.
Beats who?
Beats me.

Knock, knock.
Who's there?
Kenya.
Kenya who?
Kenya feel the love tonight?

Knock, knock.
Who's there?
Ida.
Ida who?
It's actually pronounced "Idaho."

Knock, knock.
Who's there?
Cabbage.
Cabbage who?
You expect a cabbage to have a last name?

Knock, knock.
Who's there?
Sweden.
Sweden who?
Sweden sour chicken.

Knock, knock.
Who's there?
Art.
Art who?
R2-D2!

Knock, knock.
Who's there?
Yah.
Yah who?
Take it easy there, cowboy.

Knock, knock.
Who's there?
A dolf.
A dolf who?
A dolf ball hit me in the mouth and now I can't pronounce "g."

Knock, knock.
Who's there?
Cows say.
Cows say who?
No, cows say moo.

Knock, knock.
Who's there?
Olive.
Olive who?
Olive you very much!

Knock, knock.
Who's there?
Tank.
Tank who?
You're welcome.

5

MIC DROP ONE-LINERS & MORE

JUST LIKE THE SHOVEL, MIC DROPS WERE A
GROUNDBREAKING INVENTION. THESE ARE PUNS,
ONE-LINERS, AND MAYBE TWO- OR THREE-LINERS. IF
YOU'RE LOOKING FOR YOUR AUDIENCE TO SAY "BA-DUM
TSH" OR IF YOU ARE THE KIND OF VISIONARY WHO SAYS
"BA-DUM TSH" AFTER YOUR OWN PUNCH LINE, THIS IS
THE DAD JOKE FORMAT FOR YOU. THEY'RE ALSO SOME
OF OUR FAMILY FAVORITES.

A bear walks into a bar and says, "Can I have fries . . . and . . . a cola." The bartender looks at him and says, "Why the big pause?" The bear says, "I dunno—I was born with 'em."

When the grocery store clerk asks me if I want the milk in a bag, I always tell him, "No, I'd rather drink it out of the carton!"

If you boil a funny bone it creates a laughingstock.

The rotation of Earth really makes my day.

Yesterday, I saw a guy spill all his Scrabble game pieces on the road. I asked him, "So what's the word on the street?"

Helvetica and Times New Roman walk into a bar. "Get outta here," the bartender yells. "We don't serve your type!"

After dinner, my wife asked if I could clear the table. I needed a running start, but I made it!

Did you hear Mary Poppins will no longer endorse cheap lipstick? It crumbles easily and makes her breath smell. She explained, "The super color fragile lipstick gives me halitosis."

Bad puns are how eye roll.

I accidentally handed my wife a glue stick instead of a ChapStick. She still isn't talking to me.

I like waiters—they bring a lot to the table.

I don't play soccer because I enjoy the sport. I'm just doing it for kicks.

Five-fourths of people admit they're bad with fractions.

I love jokes about eyes. The cornea the better.

On some mornings, I wake up Grumpy.
On others I let him sleep in.

I'm going to stand outside, so if anyone
asks, tell them I'm outstanding.

You should always knock on the
refrigerator before opening it just
in case there's a salad dressing.

A guy tried to sell me a mirror, but I knew
it was a scam. I could see right through it.

I once ate a dictionary and it gave me
thesaurus throat I've ever had.

My three favorite things are eating
my family and not using commas.

You know what actually makes me
smile? My facial muscles.

I am reading a horror story in braille.
Something bad is going to happen, I can feel it.

I spent $100 on a new belt that didn't even
fit. My son said it was a huge waist.

I hate it when people say age is only a
number. "Age" is clearly a word.

I have this strange talent that
I can always guess what's inside a
wrapped present. It's a gift.

Sundays are always a little sad,
but the day before is a Saturday.

To whoever stole my copy of Microsoft
Office, I will find you. You have my Word!

I left my old partner because she was obsessed
with counting. I wonder what she's up to now?

Singing in the shower is all fun and
games until you get shampoo in your
mouth. Then it's a soap opera.

I went to the store to pick up eight
cans of Sprite. When I got home,
I realized I'd only picked 7UP.

I purchased a deodorant stick today.
The instructions say, "Remove cap and
push up bottom." I can hardly walk but
when I toot, the room smells lovely.

There are three types of people: Those who can count and those who can't.

My wife changed a lot when she went vegan. It's like I never knew herbivore.

To the person who stole my glasses: I will use my contacts to find you.

I know a lot of jokes about retired people, but none of them work.

Two years ago, my doctor told me I was going deaf. I haven't heard from him since.

As I suspected, someone has been adding soil to my garden. The plot thickens.

I don't want to brag, but I finished the puzzle in a week, and it said "2 to 4 years" on the box.

Dark is spelled with a "K" and not a "C"
because you can't C in the dark.

I was gonna tell a time-traveling joke,
but you guys didn't make in time.

I was driving my bread car and it
caught fire. Now it's toast.

I just swapped our bed for a trampoline,
and my wife hit the roof.

I'm afraid of elevators, so I'm
taking steps to avoid them.

I wanted to be a doctor, but
I didn't have the patients.

A man walked into a bar. Ouch.

"RAISING KIDS MAY BE A THANKLESS
JOB WITH RIDICULOUS HOURS, BUT AT
LEAST THE PAY SUCKS."

—JIM GAFFIGAN

I was addicted to the hokey pokey, but thankfully, I turned myself around.

Don't spell "part" backward. It's a trap.

I just flew in from New York and boy are my arms tired.

I heard Cinderella tried out for the basketball team, but she kept running away from the ball.

Dear Algebra, stop trying to find your X. They're never coming back—don't ask Y.

Thanks for explaining the word "many" to me—it means a lot.

I'm on a seafood diet. Every time I see food, I eat it.

IT'S A DAD THING

BEFORE HAVING A KID, THE MOST IMPORTANT QUESTION YOU CAN ASK YOURSELF IS, "AM I PREPARED TO WATCH THE EXACT SAME EPISODE OF THE EXACT SAME CARTOON ON REPEAT FOR THE NEXT FOUR YEARS?"

I'll do algebra, I'll do trig. I'll even do statistics. But graphing is where I draw the line.

I just found out I'm color-blind. The diagnosis came completely out of the purple.

I've had amnesia for as long as I can

If at first you don't succeed, skydiving is not for you.

Today, my son asked, "Can I have a bookmark?" and I burst into tears. He's 11 years old, and he still doesn't know my name.

If a child refuses to sleep during nap time, are they guilty of resisting a rest?

I got so excited about spring
that I wet my plants.

If you see a robbery at an Apple Store,
does that make you an iWitness?

When you ask a dad if he's all
right: "No, I'm half left."

A termite walks into a bar and asks,
"Is the bar tender here?"

When a woman is giving birth,
she is literally kidding.

A ham sandwich walks into a bar and
orders a beer. The bartender says,
"Sorry, we don't serve food here."

I'm only familiar with 25 letters in the English language. I don't know Y.

As a lumberjack, I know that I've cut exactly 2,417 trees. I know because every time I cut one, I keep a log.

I had a dream that I was a muffler last night. I woke up exhausted!

My wife is really mad at the fact that I have no sense of direction. So, I packed up my stuff and right!

I don't trust stairs. They're always up to something.

I've got a great joke about construction, but I'm still working on it.

IT'S A DAD THING

CURRENTLY HELPING MY DAUGHTER
SEARCH FOR HER CHOCOLATE
THAT I ATE LAST NIGHT.

I used to hate facial hair, but
then it grew on me.

I decided to sell my vacuum cleaner—it
was just collecting dust!

I had a neck brace fitted years ago
and I've never looked back since.

You know, people say they pick their nose,
but I feel like I was just born with mine.

Some people say it's inappropriate
to make a dad joke if you're not a
dad. They call it a faux pa.

I wanted to go on a diet, but I feel like I have
way too much on my plate right now.

MY PARENTS USED TO STUFF
ME WITH CANDY WHEN I WAS A KID. M&M'S, JUJUBES,
SWEETARTS. I DON'T THINK THEY WANTED A CHILD;
I THINK THEY WANTED A PIÑATA.

—WENDY LIEBMAN

I used to work in a shoe recycling shop. It was sole-crushing.

My son screeched, "Daaaaaad, you haven't listened to one word I've said, have you!?" What a strange way to start a conversation with me.

My friend keeps saying, "Cheer up. It could be worse. You could be stuck underground in a hole full of water." I know he means well.

I ordered a chicken and an egg online. I'll let you know which one comes first.

Two cannibals are eating a clown. One says to the other, "Does this taste funny to you?"

I'm thinking about removing my spine. I feel like it's only holding me back.

My son accused me of having zero empathy. I don't understand how he can feel that way.

My daughter told me I need to stop behaving like a flamingo, so I had to put my foot down.

I like telling Dad jokes. Sometimes he laughs!

The largest knight at King Arthur's round table was Sir Cumference. He acquired his size from too much pi.

Money can't buy happiness, but it sure makes misery easier to live with.

If flying is so safe, why do they call the airport the terminal?

I don't approve of political jokes . . . I've seen too many of them get elected.

I GAVE MY FATHER $100 AND SAID, "BUY YOURSELF
SOMETHING THAT WILL MAKE YOUR LIFE EASIER."
SO HE WENT OUT AND BOUGHT A PRESENT
FOR MY MOTHER.

—RITA RUDNER

Snowmen fall from Heaven unassembled.

I got so angry the other day when
I couldn't find my stress ball.

Every night at 11:11, I make a wish that
someone will come fix my broken clock.

I'm not indecisive. Unless you want me to be.

Did you know that moths can
swim the butterfly stroke?

I'm just itching to tell you about my allergies.

I was listening to some inspirational CDs
in the car. They kept telling me to go the
extra mile. So I did, and I got lost.

The teacher said, "I can't see my pupils."

A day without sunshine is like night.

When everything's coming your
way, you're in the wrong lane.

If you can't convince them, confuse them.

Whenever I find the key to success,
someone changes the lock.

Why is the person who invests all
your money called a broker?

I just let my mind wander, and
it didn't come back.

IRS: We've got what it takes
to take what you got.

I can handle pain until it hurts.

Time flies like an arrow; fruit
flies like a banana.

When tempted to fight fire with fire, remember
that the Fire Department usually uses water.

Two guys walk into a bar; the third one ducks.

I used to work for a soft drink can crushing
company. It was soda pressing.

When you have a bladder
infection, urine trouble.

I have a fear of speed bumps, but
I'm slowly getting over it.

I was driving down the highway and a bug hit my windshield. Bet that bug doesn't have the guts to do that again.

The server asked me if I wanted my soup in a cup or a bowl, and I said, "That's a great idea, I don't like to lick it straight off the table."

My doctor asked me if I smoke, and I said, "Only when I'm on fire."

Sheep don't have cell phones—they all use lamb lines.

If you're looking for a cemetery on a map, you'll see it's dead center.

My wife told me I had to take all my penguins to the zoo. It was a great idea, and tomorrow we're going to the beach.

FATHER'S DAY IS IMPORTANT BECAUSE, BESIDES BEING
THE DAY ON WHICH WE HONOR DAD, IT'S THE ONE DAY
OF THE YEAR THAT BROOKSTONE DOES ANY BUSINESS.

—JIMMY FALLON

The clerk in the wallpaper store said
I could put it on myself, but I think
it'll look better on the wall.

A gazelle can jump higher than the
average house, because they have very
long legs and houses can't jump.

My son does his multiplication
homework on the floor because his
teacher told him not to use tables.

I don't know much about Switzerland,
but the flag is a big plus.

Unfortunately, the butcher backed
into the meat grinder and got a
little behind in his work.

Saturday and Sunday are the strongest days. The rest are weekdays.

If you want to talk to giants, you should use big words.

Humpty-Dumpty had a great fall. I'm happy for him because he had a really bad summer.

After school, all the elf children do their gnome work.

All burglars are sensitive because they take things personally.

Mummies have very discerning taste in music. They only listen to wrap.

When you die, the last parts of your body to stop working are your pupils. They dilate.

If you want to get a farm girl to like you, my advice is a tractor.

The loudest pet you can get is probably a trumpet.

All my socks have holes in them. That's how I get my feet in.

I saw the world's largest pickle, and it was a really big dill.

Two drums and a cymbal fell off a cliff. Ba-dum tsh.

WHERE THERE'S A WILL, THERE'S A RELATIVE.

—RICKY GERVAIS

BONUS:

RIDDLE ME THIS, DAD-MAN

SOME DAD JOKES SOUND LIKE RIDDLES AND SOME
RIDDLES ARE SO TOUGH THEY'RE A JOKE. KIDS LOVE
TO DO RIDDLES—EVEN SOMETIMES WITH THEIR DEAR
OLD DAD. THERE'S NOTHING BETTER THAN WATCHING
THE LOOK ON THE FACE OF A KID WHEN YOU'VE REALLY
STUMPED THEM. (IF YOU YOURSELF GET STUMPED, THE
ANSWER KEY IS IN THE BACK.)

1. I speak without a mouth and hear without ears. I have no body, but I come alive with wind. What am I?

2. You measure my life in hours and I serve you by expiring. The wind is my enemy. What am I?

3. I have cities, but no houses. I have mountains, but no trees. I have water, but no fish. What am I?

4. What is seen in the middle of March and April that can't be seen at the beginning or end of either month?

5. You see a boat filled with people. It has not sunk, but when you look again you don't see a single person on the boat. Why?

6. What word in the English language does the following: The first two letters refer to a male, the first three letters refer to a female, the first four letters refer to a great person, while the entire word refers to a great woman. What is the word?

7. I come from a mine and get surrounded by wood. Everyone uses me. What am I?

8. I weigh nothing, but you can still see me. If you put me in a bucket, I make the bucket lighter. What am I?

9. What comes once in a minute, twice in a moment, but never in a thousand years?

10. What belongs to you, but is used more by others?

11. A plane crashes on the border of the United States and Canada. Where do they bury the survivors?

12. On a freezing winter day, you enter a room that contains a lamp, a kerosene heater, and a wood burning stove. What do you light first?

13. What type of cheese is made backward?

14. What is as big as an elephant, but weighs nothing?

15. In a one-story pink house, there was a pink person, a pink cat, a pink fish, a pink computer, a pink chair, a pink table, a pink telephone, a pink shower—everything was pink! What color were the stairs?

16. Two mothers and three daughters went out to eat. Everyone ate one burger, yet only three burgers were eaten in all. How was this possible?

17. A man was outside taking a walk when it started to rain. The man didn't have an umbrella and he wasn't wearing a hat. His clothes got soaked, yet not a single hair on his head got wet. How could this happen?

18. Imagine you're in a room that is filling with water. There are no windows or doors. How do you get out?

19. Name four days of the week that start with the letter "T."

20. I'm full of keys, but can't open any door. What am I?

21. What is a word comprised of four letters, occasionally written with 12 letters and later with five, never written with five, but happily with seven?

22. What starts with a "P," ends with an "E," and has thousands of letters?

23. Why do we tell actors to break a leg?

24. If you give me water, I will die. What am I?

25. Almost everyone needs it, asks for it, or gives it, but almost nobody takes it. What is it?

26. A man was driving a black truck. His lights were not on. The moon was not out. A lady was crossing the street. How did the man see her?

27. What is something you can put in your pocket that keeps it empty?

28. What gets wet when drying?

29. What has to be broken before you can use it?

30. I'm tall when I'm young, and I'm short when I'm old. What am I?

31. What month of the year has 28 days?

32. What is full of holes but still holds water?

33. What question can you never answer yes to?

34. What is always in front of you but can't be seen?

35. What can you break, even if you never pick it up or touch it?

36. What can you keep after giving to someone?

37. What's blue and smells like red paint?

38. I shave every day, but my beard stays the same. What am I?

39. I have branches, but no fruit, trunk, or leaves. What am I?

40. The more of this there is, the less you see. What is it?

41. What can you hold in your left hand but not in your right?

42. Where does today come before yesterday?

43. What invention lets you look right through a wall?

44. What has one head, one foot, and four legs?

45. What is cut on a table, but is never eaten?

46. What can you catch, but not throw?

47. What can travel all around the world without leaving its corner?

48. What has a thumb and four fingers, but is not a hand?

49. What tastes better than it smells?

Riddle Answer Key

Opener: If six children and two dogs were under a broken umbrella, how come none of them got wet?
It wasn't raining.

1. I speak without a mouth and hear without ears. I have no body, but I come alive with wind. What am I?
An echo.

2. You measure my life in hours and I serve you by expiring. The wind is my enemy. What am I?
A candle.

3. I have cities, but no houses. I have mountains, but no trees. I have water, but no fish. What am I?
A map.

4. What is seen in the middle of March and April that can't be seen at the beginning or end of either month?
The letter "R."

5. You see a boat filled with people. It has not sunk, but when you look again you don't see a single person on the boat. Why?
All the people got married.

6. What word in the English language does the following: The first two letters refer to a male, the first three letters refer to a female, the first four letters refer to a great person, while the entire word refers to a great woman. What is the word?
Heroine.

7. I come from a mine and get surrounded by wood.
   Everyone uses me. What am I?
   Pencil lead.

8. I weigh nothing, but you can still see me. If you put
   me in a bucket, I make the bucket lighter. What am I?
   A hole!

9. What comes once in a minute, twice in a moment, but
   never in a thousand years?
   The letter "M."

10. What belongs to you, but is used more by others?
    Your name.

11. A plane crashes on the border of the United States
    and Canada. Where do they bury the survivors?
    You don't bury survivors.

12. On a freezing winter day, you enter a room that
    contains a lamp, a kerosene heater, and a wood
    burning stove. What do you light first?
    A match, of course.

13. What type of cheese is made backward?
    Edam.

14. What is as big as an elephant, but weighs nothing?
    The elephant's shadow.

15. In a one-story pink house, there was a pink person,
    a pink cat, a pink fish, a pink computer, a pink chair, a
    pink table, a pink telephone, a pink shower—everything
    was pink! What color were the stairs?
    There weren't any stairs. It was a one-story house.

16. Two mothers and three daughters went out to eat. Everyone ate one burger, yet only three burgers were eaten in all. How was this possible?
They were a grandmother, her daughter, and her granddaughter.

17. A man was outside taking a walk when it started to rain. The man didn't have an umbrella and he wasn't wearing a hat. His clothes got soaked, yet not a single hair on his head got wet. How could this happen?
The man was bald.

18. Imagine you're in a room that is filling with water. There are no windows or doors. How do you get out?
Stop imagining.

19. Name four days of the week that start with the letter "T."
Tuesday, Thursday, today, and tomorrow.

20. I'm full of keys, but can't open any door. What am I?
A piano.

21. What is a word comprised of four letters, occasionally written with 12 letters and later with five, never written with five, but happily with seven?
What, Occasionally, Later, Never, Happily.

22. What starts with a "P", ends with an "E", and has thousands of letters?
The post office.

23. Why do we tell actors to break a leg?
Because every play has a cast.

24. If you give me water, I will die. What am I?
Fire.

25. Almost everyone needs it, asks for it, or gives it, but almost nobody takes it. What is it?
Advice.

26. A man was driving a black truck. His lights were not on. The moon was not out. A lady was crossing the street. How did the man see her?
It was a bright, sunny day.

27. What is something you can put in your pocket that keeps it empty?
A large hole.

28. What gets wet when drying?
A towel.

29. What has to be broken before you can use it?
An egg.

30. I'm tall when I'm young, and I'm short when I'm old. What am I?
A candle.

31. What month of the year has 28 days?
All of them.

32. What is full of holes but still holds water?
A sponge.

33. What question can you never answer yes to?
Are you asleep yet?

34. What is always in front of you but can't be seen?
    The future.

35. What can you break, even if you never pick it up or touch it?
    A promise.

36. What can you keep after giving to someone?
    Your word.

37. What's blue and smells like red paint?
    Blue paint.

38. I shave every day, but my beard stays the same. What am I?
    A barber.

39. I have branches, but no fruit, trunk, or leaves. What am I?
    A bank.

40. The more of this there is, the less you see. What is it?
    Darkness.

41. What can you hold in your left hand but not in your right?
    Your right elbow.

42. Where does today come before yesterday?
    The dictionary.

43. What invention lets you look right through a wall?
    The window.

44. What has one head, one foot, and four legs?
A bed.

45. What is cut on a table, but is never eaten?
A deck of cards.

46. What can you catch, but not throw?
A cold.

47. What can travel all around the world without leaving its corner?
A stamp.

48. What has a thumb and four fingers, but is not a hand?
A glove.

49. What tastes better than it smells?
Your tongue.

Resources

DadAndBuried.com or on Instagram at @dadandburied

DadOrAlive.com

DudeDad.com; on Instagram at @dudedad; and his book, *A Daily Dose of Dad Jokes*

Fatherly.com

HiMyNameIsMom.com and *Hi My Name Is Mom* podcast

JugglingTheJenkins.com

LifeOfDad.com or on Instagram at @lifeofdad

LifeOfMom.com or on Instagram at @lifeofmom

ScaryMommy.com

Simon Holland on Twitter at @simoncholland

TheDad.com

About the Author

Adrian Kulp has worked as a comedy booking agent for CBS, as a TV executive for Adam Sandler's Happy Madison Productions, and as vice president of development for Chelsea Handler's Borderline Amazing Productions. For the past 10 years, he's been the voice behind the popular dad blog turned parenting memoir, *Dad or Alive: Confessions of an Unexpected Stay-at-Home Dad*. He's produced the reality series *Modern Dads* for A&E Network and is a partner at the largest online fatherhood community, Life of Dad, where he works on the creative team and with branded content. Kulp is also the senior executive producer of *The Ty Bentli Show* on NASH FM.

In 2018, he wrote the first book in his parenting trilogy, *We're Pregnant! The First-Time Dad's Pregnancy Handbook*, which has been a bestseller since its debut. In 2019, he followed this up with the second book, *We're Parents! The New Dad's Guide to Baby's First Year*, and in 2020 released *We're Parenting a Toddler!* He now lives in Nashville, Tennessee, with his wife, Jen, and their four kids, Ava, Charlie, Mason, and Evelyn. This is his first joke book.